Gita Wisdom Tales

JNANA – KNOWLEDGE

Inspiring stories explaining key shlokas of the Bhagavad Gita

Gauranga Darshan Das

Om SHAKTI
An Imprint of Om Books International

Author's Note

Among all the scriptures, the Bhagavad Gita holds a special significance, since these are the words of Lord Krishna. Krishna voiced the Gita on the battlefield of Kurukshetra to motivate His dear friend and devotee, Arjuna. The Gita presents amazing truths of life and deep wisdom. However, it is not a storybook.

While sharing the Bhagavad Gita, especially with children, I found the concepts of the Gita sinking in better among children when presented with suitable stories. I have, therefore, attempted to incorporate them in the series, Gita Wisdom Tales.

The intriguing anecdotes and examples infused in the book richen its flavour, and open up a totally new dimension of the Gita for children and adults alike! These stories have been carefully selected from various scriptures, including the Srimad Bhagavatam, the Ramayana, the Mahabharata, the Puranas, biographies of great people, and even some traditional folklore, to highlight the import of 50 Bhagavad Gita shlokas, presented in five volumes. Relayed in a simple language, the Gita wisdom will surely find its way into little hearts and hearts that live young.

- Gauranga Darshan Das

Contents

Introduction: The Story of the Bhagavad Gita

Dear children! Do you know what the words 'Bhagavad Gita' mean? 'Bhagavan' means God. 'Gita' means a song. Therefore, Bhagavad Gita means the song that God has sung. Read on to know when, where, and why did God sing this divine song.

Pandu and Dhritarashtra were princes of the great empire of Hastinapur.

Dhritarashtra was Pandu's elder brother. Since Dhritarashtra was blind, Pandu became the king. Pandu had five noble sons named Yudhishthira, Bhima, Arjuna, Nakula and Sahadeva – together who were known as the Pandavas. Dhritarashtra had one hundred sons, the eldest of them being the wicked Duryodhana.

Duryodhana hated the Pandavas and tried to trouble them and kill them multiple times. He set their home on fire. He took away their kingdom by cheating in a dice game and sent them on exile for thirteen years. Even after the Pandavas completed their period of exile, Duryodhana didn't return their kingdom. So, war between them became unavoidable.

Finally, the armies of Yudhishthira and Duryodhana met on the battlefield at a holy place called Kurukshetra. Lord Krishna, the dearest friend and guide of the Pandavas, chose to drive the chariot of Arjuna during the battle. The war was about to begin.

Arjuna took up his bow but couldn't shoot arrows towards his enemies. He thought, *How can I kill my own relatives and friends?* He softened towards his cousins and other family members, whom he respected. He was confused whether he should fight, or simply give up. He gave several reasons to Krishna why he could not fight. Seeing his dear friend Arjuna immersed in deep confusion, Krishna tried motivating him. To clear the confusions in Arjuna's mind, Lord Krishna voiced the Bhagavad Gita.

Sometimes, we also get confused in our lives, while performing our duties. The Gita takes us on a journey from confusion to clarity.

Although the Gita was narrated in the context of war, there was hardly any discussion about war in the Gita. The Gita presents several lessons on how to lead a meaningful life. Through Arjuna, Lord Krishna passed on His divine teachings to humankind. So let us read the beautiful Bhagavad Gita, God's message to all of us.

This book presents some key shlokas, explained with suitable stories. Hope these wisdom tales will inspire you to read the entire Gita, when you are older.

1. THE GREATEST PERSON

मत्तः परतरं नान्यत्किञ्चिदस्ति धनञ्जय ।
मयि सर्वमिदं प्रोतं सूत्रे मणिगणा इव ॥

mattah parataram nanyat
kincid asti dhananjaya
mayi sarvam idam protam
sutre mani-gana iva ॥ 7.7 ॥

Have you ever seen a beautiful pearl necklace? What do you like the best in it? The shape of the pearls, the colour of the pearls, the golden pendant or the exquisite design? Well, the pearls and pendants are all very pretty in their own way, but, have you ever thought about what holds them together? It's the invisible string inside the pearls!

Similarly, God is the one who maintains everything and everyone within the Universe. Nobody is equal to or superior to Him. In this shloka, Lord Krishna Himself reveals: "O Arjuna, there is no one superior to Me. Everything rests upon Me, as pearls are strung on a thread."

The Lord is the source of the entire Universe. With our material eyes, we cannot see His divine form. But we can surely feel His presence by sincerely performing bhakti. Gradually, we can even see Him, when we are purified of all bad qualities.

Here are a few stories of great devotees who witnessed Krishna's potency as the Supreme Lord.

The Universe in Krishna's Mouth

One day, little Krishna was playing with His friends and brother Balarama in Vrindavan while Mother Yashoda was busy performing her household chores.

Suddenly, Balarama and Krishna's playmates ran to Mother Yashoda and began complaining, "O Mother, Krishna has eaten mud."

Mother Yashoda became worried. She caught hold of Krishna and asked him, "Why have You eaten mud? Just see, all Your friends are complaining. Even Balarama says so."

Krishna became afraid, and replied, "Mother, I never ate mud. All their complaints are simply false. My elder brother, Balarama, while playing, became angry with Me and joined the other boys. So, they all are siding against Me. If you do not believe me, then look into My mouth and check whether I have eaten mud or not."

Mother Yashoda replied, "All right, then open Your mouth wide. I shall see."

Krishna then opened His little mouth just like any ordinary boy. However, as soon as Mother Yashoda looked into His mouth, she was stunned and bewildered. Within her son's little mouth, she saw the entire creation – the outer space, planets, sun, moon, stars, mountains, islands, oceans, rivers, the devas, all species of living beings, and so on. She even saw their cowherd village of Vrindavan, along with herself and her son within Krishna's mouth.

Thus, seeing the entire Universe in her child's mouth, Mother Yashoda became astonished and scared. She thought, *Is this a dream? Or is it really true? Am I under some illusion? Or have I gone mad? Is my child so powerful? Or has He been inflicted with some disease?*

As Mother Yashoda thought thus, the all-powerful Lord Krishna, acting as a child in Vrindavan, began thinking as well, *If My mother thinks that I am God, who will cuddle and look after Me? I enjoy her scolding, feeding and other activities driven by pure motherly affection.*

By the desire of the Lord, there was an immediate transformation in Mother Yashoda, as she forgot everything she had just seen. Once again, she took Krishna on her lap and smothered Him with motherly love, with no recollection of the divine vision she had seen in little Krishna's mouth.

Krishna, though the Supreme Creator, enjoys being a child of His dear devotee.

Arjuna Sees Krishna's Vishva-rupa

While singing the Bhagavad Gita to Arjuna, Lord Krishna said, "I am the source of the entire Universe, everything emanates from Me and is dependent on Me. Knowing this, My devotees serve Me with full dedication."

Arjuna asked, "My dear Krishna, You are the Supreme God. Please explain to me your divine power."

Krishna replied, "O Arjuna, I am the Supersoul (Paramatma) in the heart of all living beings. I am the beginning, the middle and the end of everything. I am the sun among the luminaries, I am the moon among the stars. I am Indra among the devas, I am the mind among the senses. I am the Meru among the mountains, I am the ocean among the water bodies. I am the banyan tree among the trees, I am the Ananta among many hooded snakes. I am the Ganga among the rivers. In this way, there is no end to My grandeur. What I have spoken to you is a mere indication of My infinite power. Anything beautiful, powerful and majestic in this world is just a small fragment of My power. I am everywhere in the Universe, and support it with My divine energy."

Krishna continued, "O Arjuna, I grant you divine vision to witness My Vishva-rupa in which everything in the entire Universe is visible at one place."

Arjuna then saw unlimited Krishnas shining brighter than a thousand suns. He could see the sages, devas, humans, animals, birds, and all species of life. He bowed before Krishna and said, "O Lord, I see in Your body Brahma, Shiva, the sages, divine serpents and all living beings. I see no end, no middle, no beginning of this form.

You are touching the sky with many radiant colours, huge mouths and glowing eyes. I see that all the sons of Dhritarashtra, Bhishma, Drona, Karna and other chief warriors are rushing into Your blazing mouths like moths entering fire to meet their death. I treated You like my friend not knowing Your glory. I am fearful upon seeing Your Vishva-rupa. Kindly withdraw this form and show me Your pleasant four -handed form as Vishnu."

Krishna then revealed His four-armed form as Vishnu, and later His two-handed form as Lord Krishna. Arjuna then regained his composure and was prepared to fight.

Krishna is omnipresent, and everything in the Universe stems from Him.

Lord Krishna is the source of everything in the Universe, as He showed to Mother Yashoda and Arjuna. But He also enjoys friendly exchanges with His devotees. He is a combination of supreme greatness and supreme sweetness.

2. WHEN DOES GOD APPEAR?

यदा यदा हि धर्मस्य ग्लानिर्भवति भारत।
अभ्युत्थानमधर्मस्य तदात्मानं सृजाम्यहम्॥

yada yada hi dharmasya
glanir bhavati bharata
abhyutthanam adharmasya
tadatmanam srijamyaham ॥ 4.7 ॥

The Lord comes to this world from His spiritual abode out of kindness and compassion for the people suffering here. But when does He exactly descend?

Lord Krishna reveals, "Whenever there is a decline in righteousness (dharma) and whenever there is an increase in unrighteousness (adharma), I come to the Earth in some form, to reverse the situation."

Dharma or righteousness stands on four pillars namely – truthfulness (*satyam*), cleanliness (*saucham*), kindness (*daya*), and austerity (*tapa*). And adharma or unrighteousness flourishes due to negative qualities like envy, pride, anger, greed, and so on. So, whenever people on Earth take to adharma and neglect dharma, the Lord comes to Earth in a befitting form to teach and establish dharma.

Bhumi Devi's Distress

Once the goddess of Earth – Bhumi Devi was in deep distress. The kings ruling the Earth at that time were demoniac, cruel and mean. Their gigantic armies troubled innocent people. As a result of such adharma, Mother Earth was overburdened.

Unable to tolerate this, Bhumi Devi went to Lord Brahma with tears in her eyes. She took the form of a cow, and told Brahma about her distress due to the demoniac kings. Seeing her weeping helplessly, Brahma became compassionate. He at once took her to the *Ksheer Sagar*, or the ocean of milk, where Lord Vishnu resides. Lord Brahma also took several devas like Shiva and Indra with him.

Together, they arrived at the shore of the ocean of milk, which was located on the planet called Sveta-dvipa. Then, all of them began offering prayers to please Lord Vishnu. They also recited the *Purusha Sukta*.

Still, they did not receive any response from Lord Vishnu. Brahma then started meditating on the Lord who in reply transmitted a message to Brahma from within his heart. Even at the beginning of creation, Lord Vishnu had taught all the Vedas to Brahma from within Brahma's heart.

Having thus received the message, Brahma then announced to all present there, "The Supreme Lord Krishna will very soon appear on Earth in the Yadu dynasty. He will destroy adharma by punishing the demons, and will protect dharma by protecting the righteous devotees. All of you devas and your wives also should appear on the Earth in different dynasties, to assist Lord Krishna in His mission. Lord Krishna would personally appear as the son of Vasudeva. Lord Ananta (Balarama), an expansion of Lord Krishna, would also appear as His elder brother."

After informing all the *devas* and consoling Bhumi Devi with sweet words, Lord Brahma returned to his planet Brahmaloka. Soon after, Lord Krishna appeared on the Earth and destroyed adharma by killing many demons like Putana, Vatsasur, Aghasur, Vyomasura, Arishtasur, Narakasur, and so on. Thus He relieved Bhumi from her distress and established dharma on this planet. He also delivered wonderful teachings in the form of the *Bhagavad Gita*.

The Lord appears to relieve His devotees from distress.

Lord Varaha Kills Hiranyaksha

Hiranyaksha and Hiranyakashipu were two cruel demons, the sons of Sage Kashyapa. Owing to severe austerities, Hiranyaksha received boons from Lord Brahma and became very strong. Desperate to fight, he started searching all over the Universe for a combatant of equal calibre. Seeing his temper and power, even the devas in heaven got frightened and fled.

After terrorising the devas, Hiranyaksha dived deep into an ocean. Striking the waves of the ocean with his powerful mace, he scared away all the creatures of the sea. Seeing the Lord of the Waters, Varuna, Hiranyaksha fell at his feet and sarcastically said, "Oh great warrior, please agree to battle with me."

Observing his false humility, Varuna replied, "O great warrior, I have become old now, and I can't match your strength. Only Lord Vishnu can satisfy your wish to fight. Only He can slash all your pride and make you lie low on the battlefield to be devoured by dogs. He mercifully appears in several incarnations to punish wicked men like you, and establish dharma."

Hiranyaksha then went out in search of Lord Vishnu. On the way, he met Narada Muni and asked him, "Do you know where Lord Vishnu resides?" Narada replied, "You can go to Garbhodaka ocean. There you will find Lord Vishnu elegantly seated on His snake bed."

Hiranyaksha angrily marched to the Garbhodaka ocean. On reaching, he saw a great boar bearing the Earth on His tusks. Hiranyaksha laughed and said, "Oh beast, this Earth is ours. You cannot take it as long as I am here. Fight me, if at all you have any courage. Today I will kill you." So saying, Hiranyaksha began to chase Lord Varaha.

The Goddess of Earth, Bhumi Devi, who was on the tusks of Varaha became scared. Lord Varaha then placed Bhumi Devi on the surface of the water, and gave her the ability to float. All the devas assembled around, anxiously waiting to see what would follow.

Lord Varaha angrily replied, "O demon! As you said, we are denizens of the jungle, searching for dogs like you. Certainly, I will stay here as you have asked. I will not leave before I display My power. Give up your foolish talk and prepare to fight."

Being thus challenged, Hiranyaksha became as angry as a lion. He quickly sprung upon the Lord and gave Him a blow with his powerful mace. Hiranyaksha hissed like a snake and bit his lips. The Lord effortlessly knocked his mace down.

The Lord then challenged Hiranyaksha, "Take up your weapon once again and try conquering Me." Hiranyaksha then invoked the deadly trident and hurled it at the Lord. The Lord cut it to pieces with His Sudarshan Chakra.

Hiranyaksha then created several demonic illusions, like fierce winds and clouds accompanied by lightning and thunder. He created a mystic mountain that rained pus, blood, stool, urine and bones. Different rakshasas started emerging and began voicing violent slogans. But Lord Varaha effortlessly destroyed all the illusions with His Sudarshan Chakra.

Frustrated, Hiranyaksha started to strike the Lord's chest with his hard fists. The Lord then slapped him at the root of his ear and Hiranyaksha's eyeballs bulged out. His arms and legs were broken, his head ripped off, and he fell down like an uprooted tree.

Seeing the demon's dead body, Brahma admired the Lord and offered prayers. Bhumi Devi on Lord Varaha's tusks appeared like a lotus flower being held by an elephant with its trunk. In this way, the Lord protected Mother Earth from demons like Hiranyaksha.

The Lord punishes demoniac people who possess qualities like anger, pride and greed.

When Bhumi Devi was distressed due to demoniac rulers like Hiranyaksha, the Lord Himself appeared in the form of Krishna and Lord Varaha, to relieve her of her distress. If we cultivate the qualities that foster dharma within ourselves, the Lord will respond to our calls and vanquish our difficulties.

3. WHEN DOES GOD APPEAR?

परित्राणाय साधुनां विनाशाय च दुष्कृताम् ।
धर्मसंस्थानार्थाय सम्भवामि युगे युगे ॥

paritranaya sadhunam
vinashaya cha dushkritam
dharma-sansthapanarthaya
sambhavami yuge yuge ॥ 4.8 ॥

Now we know *when* Krishna appears but, wouldn't it be great to know *why* He appears?

In this shloka, Krishna describes why He comes to Earth in different forms at different times. He says, "I appear on this planet in every yuga for three reasons – Firstly, to protect the righteous, secondly, to punish the wicked, and thirdly, to establish dharma."

But, how can the Lord protect some people and punish others? He is the Father of everyone and must be equal to all, isn't it? Yes. Krishna being the Supreme Father, considers everyone as equal. But, only some of His children obey Him, while others act against Him. So, the Lord treats them as per their actions.

Krishna primarily comes to this world to protect His devotees. Punishing the demons is a secondary reason. So let's see how the Lord protected some of His greatest devotees from some of the greatest demons.

Krishna Kills Kamsa and Protects His Parents

Once in Mathura, King Kamsa had arranged for a grand wrestling festival. Desiring to kill Krishna, he invited Him to Mathura on the pretext of the festival. The city-dwellers and visitors from nearby places sat in the galleries while Kamsa took his seat on the royal dais. At the entrance of the wrestling arena, Kamsa had stationed a mighty elephant named Kuvalayapida to attack Krishna.

Krishna arrived along with His brother Balarama just before the start of the event. The enormous Kuvalayapida struck Krishna hard. But Krishna struck him back and hid among his legs. Kuvalayapida sought Krishna out with his sense of smell. But Krishna teased and tormented the elephant till it was mad with rage. Eventually, He pulled out one of his tusks, and with that very tusk He beat the elephant to death.

Adorned with the blood of Kuvalayapida and carrying his tusk on His shoulder, the invincible Krishna entered the wrestling arena of Kamsa. The residents of Mathura were mesmerised by Krishna's beauty and started praising Him.

Kamsa then ordered his powerful wrestlers Chanura and Mushtika to attack Krishna

and Balarama. The audience, especially the women, felt compassionate towards the charming boys, and found it unfair. Vasudeva and Devaki became anxious when they saw their sons being attacked by the strong wrestlers.

To encourage all the people who were concerned about them, Krishna and Balarama displayed their strength and expertise in wrestling. Chanura and Mushtika were soon defeated. They could not stand up to the boys.

Everyone, except Kamsa rejoiced. In mad rage, Kamsa commanded, "Arrest and kill Vasudeva, Nanda, Ugrasena and all the cowherds." Krishna became furious and instantly jumped onto the elevated royal dais. Kamsa took his sword and shield and moved swiftly like a hawk. Krishna, however, grabbed Kamsa by his hair, and hurled him down into the wrestling ring. He then jumped atop his chest. Striking him with His bare fists, Krishna killed him. The villagers were liberated from a reign of terror. Kamsa too attained liberation through death and thus fulfilled his destiny.

Krishna then released His parents Devaki and Vasudeva and reinstated His grandfather, Ugrasena, as King of Mathura.

Parashurama Kills the Proud Kshatriyas

Once in the kingdom of the Haihayas, there lived a powerful king named Kartaviryarjuna. His capital city was Mahishmati. He had received 1,000 arms as a result of his worship of Lord Dattatreya. He was very proud of his power.

One day, while on a hunt, Kartaviryarjuna entered a forest. While moving in the forest, he came across the hermitage of Sage Jamadagni. The sage welcomed the king, his soldiers and ministers. He treated them very well and arranged for all their comforts.

Kartaviryarjuna was amazed to see such hospitality. He wondered how a simple sage living in a forest could arrange such elaborate facilities for thousands of his soldiers. He then found that Jamadagni had a mystic cow named Kamadhenu who supplied whatever he needed.

Kartaviryarjuna became envious and wanted Kamadhenu for himself. He then forcibly took away the cow along with her calf to his capital Mahishmati. Jamadagni, being a brahmana sage, was rendered helpless.

Jamadagni had a powerful son named Parashurama, who was indeed Lord Vishnu incarnate. Hearing about Kartaviryarjuna's sinful act of stealing a cow from a brahmana, Parashurama became as furious as an injured tiger. Taking up his fierce axe, bow and arrows, he chased Kartaviryarjuna just like a tiger chases a deer.

Parashurama was a fearful sight in deerskin and matted locks of hair that shone like the sun. Kartaviryarjuna sent thousands of his men equipped with clubs, swords, arrows, weapons, elephants, chariots, and horses, to fight Parashurama. But Lord Parashurama

single-handedly killed them all. At the speed of the mind and wind, Lord Parashurama wielded his axe and sliced off their legs, arms and necks. He killed the whole army including drivers, carriers, elephants and horses. The ground was covered with their blood.

Seeing this, Kartaviryarjuna rushed to the battlefield. With his 1,000 arms, he fixed arrows on 500 bows to kill Parashurama. But Parashurama released enough arrows with only one bow and cut to pieces all the arrows and bows Kartaviryarjuna had. Kartaviryarjuna then uprooted many trees, picked up heavy rocks and hurled them towards Parashurama. But Parashurama dodged them all and cut off the thousand arms of Kartaviryarjuna with his axe. Eventually he beheaded Kartaviryarjuna.

Kartaviryarjuna had 10,000 sons. Seeing their father's death, all of them fled in fear. Then Parashurama brought back Kamadhenu and her calf, and returned them to Jamadagni. Jamadagni then spoke to Parashurama, "We are brahmanas. We should forgive people, and not kill them. Killing is a sin. So, to purify yourself of the sin, you should go for a pilgrimage for one year." Parashurama obediently followed his father's order.

Thereafter, to revenge their father's death, the sons of Kartaviryarjuna arrived at Jamadagni's hermitage, in the absence of Parashurama. They saw Jamadagni meditating on Lord Vishnu and cut off his head ruthlessly. Jagamadagni's wife Renuka loudly cried out in pain, "O Parashurama, my dear son!"

Parashurama, although far away, heard her cry, and rushed there at once. Seeing his father's dead body, he took up his axe. Having decided to put an end to all the proud kshatriyas, he went to Mahishmati, and killed the 10,000 sons of Kartaviryarjuna making a mountain of their chopped heads in the middle of the city.

A river of blood flowed there causing fear in those who disrespected the brahmanas. Parashurama then killed several such sinful kshatriyas 21 times, and created 9 lakes with their blood at Samanta-Panchaka. Later, Parashurama affixed his father's head to his dead body, and revived him.

The Lord doesn't tolerate any offence against devotees.

Vasudeva and Devaki were virtuous, and so was Sage Jamadagni. Therefore, the Lord could not tolerate the offences of Kamsa and the proud kshatriyas against His devotees and thus killed them. If we too devote ourselves unto Krishna fully, He will protect us from the dangers that come our way.

4. IS GOD PARTIAL?

समोऽहं सर्वभूतेषु न मे द्वेष्योऽस्ति न प्रियः ।
ये भजन्ति तु मां भक्त्या मयि ते तेषु चाप्यहम् ॥

samo 'ham sarva-bhuteshu
na me dveshyo 'sti na priyah
ye bhajanti tu mam bhaktya
mayi te teshu capy aham ॥ 9.29 ॥

Have you ever wondered why some people are rich, and others poor? Some are happy while others are sad? Is it due to God's partiality? After all, if everyone is God's child, how can He be partial to anyone? Let's hear the answer from Krishna directly.

In this shloka, Lord Krishna says, "I am equal to everyone. I envy no one, nor am I ever partial to anyone. However, I show some special favour to those who worship and serve Me with devotion. I consider such selfless and dedicated devotees as My dear friends."

Let's consider the example of a mother with her two children. To this loving mother both her children are equal. But she will treat them as per their behaviour.

Lord Krishna, also loves all His children. But He deals with different people in different ways. He protects His devotees who are righteous while punishing the wicked who act immorally.

Arjuna vs. Duryodhana

Before the war of Kurukshetra, Duryodhana wanted to meet Krishna personally to seek His assistance in the war. Arjuna, the dearest devotee, friend and cousin of Krishna, also decided to go personally to seek Krishna's help. When Arjuna reached Krishna's palace, he saw Krishna's guards receiving Duryodhana, who had just arrived. The two princes greeted each other and entered Krishna's chamber together. They found Krishna asleep while one of His wives was fanning Him gently.

Duryodhana went straight to the head of the bed and sat there, but Arjuna stood at Krishna's lotus feet with folded palms. While Arjuna gazed at Krishna's face, tears of love rolled down his cheeks. After a while, Krishna woke up. As He opened His eyes and sat up, His eyes

fell on Arjuna first. Krishna later saw Duryodhana who was actually behind His back now. He welcomed both and inquired the purpose of their visit.

Duryodhana said, “I have come here to seek Your assistance in the war. I arrived before Arjuna. So, it is only right that You assist me rather than him.” Krishna smiled and said, “I agree that you arrived first, but I saw Arjuna first. Further, the scriptures say that one should help the youngest first, so I will first offer My assistance to Arjuna, who is younger to you.” Duryodhana became somewhat upset seeing Krishna’s partiality.

Krishna then said, “I have an army of one million soldiers called Narayani-sena, who are all equal to Me in battle. One of you may take them and the other may take Me. But I will not fight. I will not take up arms throughout the battle. O Arjuna, what do you choose?” Hearing this, Duryodhana became anxious. He was afraid that Arjuna would choose the invincible army. How would an unarmed Krishna be of use during the war?

To his surprise, Arjuna said, “Krishna, I want you. Your presence is more precious to me than any army.”

Duryodhana's joy knew no bounds, and he could hardly conceal his joy. He thought, *Arjuna is sentimental, and not intelligent. He has forsaken a powerful army and preferred Krishna, who would not even fight. What foolishness!* Smiling mildly, Duryodhana said, "It seems then that I am left with the army. I shall accept it." He then took Krishna's leave and departed.

Evil Duryodhana neither had love for Krishna nor faith in His divine presence, while Arjuna had both profusely. Krishna showcased these qualities of Arjuna and Duryodhana by apparently displaying partiality to Arjuna. Actually, Krishna simply reciprocated the love and devotion of Arjuna.

God is not partial; He is reciprocal. He will respond based on how we approach Him.

Mohini Murti Favours the Devas

Once, the asuras (demons) defeated the devas and occupied heaven. Having no other way to regain their positions, the devas approached Lord Vishnu for advice and support. Whenever the devas get into trouble, it is the Supreme Lord Vishnu who rescues them.

Lord Vishnu explained, "My dear devas, please go to the asuras and make an agreement with them. Together, you must churn the milk ocean by making the Mandara Mountain the churning rod, and Vasuki, the serpent, the churning rope. In this way you will get amrit (nectar) which will give you longevity and strength. Please be patient with the asuras, and agree with their demands, as they are more powerful than you at present."

The devas followed the advice of Lord Vishnu and churned the milk ocean (*Ksheer Sagar*) with the asuras. Lord Vishnu assisted them in many ways in this effort. Finally, when the amrit was collected, the asuras took the pot of amrit and ran away. Then the asuras started quarrelling among themselves for the first share of the amrit.

The devas were left in disappointment. Lord Vishnu consoled them, and took the form of a beautiful woman. The form is known as Mohini Murti. (S)he then went before the asuras. Seeing Mohini, the asuras were dumbfounded. They trusted her because somehow, each asura thought that Mohini loved him alone. They all requested her to take up the responsibility of amrit distribution. Mohini agreed and told all the devas and asuras to get in queues.

Mohini first went to the asuras and beguiled them with her sweet words and gestures. She then began distributing all the amrit to the devas to provide them longevity and immortality. The asuras remained silent as they were unwilling to fight with a charming woman and spoil their chances of impressing her.

But one of the asuras named Raahu disguised himself as a deva and drank some amrit secretly. The Sun-God (Surya) and the Moon-God (Chandra) detected him and informed Mohini. Mohini, who was none other than Vishnu himself, at once cut off Raahu's head with the Sudarshan Chakra (disc weapon) before the amrit could enter his body. But Raahu's head, being touched by amrit, became immortal. To take revenge, Raahu is believed to attack Surya and Chandra. These attacks are popularly known as solar and lunar eclipses.

After distributing all the amrit among the devas, Mohini disappeared. In this way, the devas became powerful, and regained their positions in heaven. Although the asuras also worked hard to churn the milk ocean and produce amrit, they didn't get even a single drop. This, however, was not due to Lord Vishnu's partiality or injustice, but His natural reciprocation towards the devotion of the devas, and justice against the scheming asuras who had run away with the amrit. Further, it would have been very dangerous to give amrit to the asuras, who were inherently evil and envious. They would unnecessarily trouble the innocent, including children, women, brahmans and cows. Had the asuras received amrit, havoc would have reigned the Universe. Hence, the Lord prevented them from having amrit.

The Lord ensures that people get what they deserve.

The Lord reciprocated Arjuna's and the devas' love, while He treated Duryodhana and the demons differently. On similar lines, if we approach Him with love and respect, we can experience loving reciprocations from Him. Read the next shloka and the stories for a deeper understanding.

5. HOW DOES KRISHNA RECIPROCATE?

ये यथा मां प्रपद्यन्ते तांस्तथैव भजाम्यहम्।
मम वर्त्मानुवर्तन्ते मनुष्याः पार्थ सर्वशः॥

ye yatha mam prapadyante
tams tathaiva bhajamy aham
mama vartmanuvartante
manusyah partha sarvasah ॥ 4.11 ॥

Isn't it natural for you to befriend someone who behaves in a friendly manner with you? Similarly, wouldn't you deal differently with a person who behaves rudely with you?

In this shloka Krishna says, "I respond to people as per the way they approach Me. I reward them according to their actions.. Everyone follows My path, whether they do it consciously or unconsciously."

Here are the stories of two people - one who dealt with Krishna rudely and one who dealt with Him lovingly. Let us see the outcomes.

The Arrogant Washerman

Lord Krishna was born in Mathura, but He spent His childhood in Vrindavan. After spending many eventful years with the gopas, the gopis and cows at Vrindavan, and performing various miracles, Krishna returned to His birthplace, Mathura.

On entering the city, Krishna and His elder brother Balarama met a washerman carrying colourful clothes for Kamsa, the cruel king of Mathura. Krishna politely asked him, "Dear washerman, we are cowherds coming from Vrindavan. Can you please give us some clothes? We desire to wear the beautiful garments that you are carrying. I promise you that you will be greatly blessed by offering us suitable clothes."

What fortune! While millions of devotees eagerly wait for an opportunity to offer something

to the Lord, Krishna Himself was asking the washerman for some clothes.

Instead of recognising his good fortune, the proud washerman replied arrogantly, "How dare you ask for the king's clothes? You are an uncivilised, poor cowherd. Do you think you deserve to wear such expensive garments? If you dare ask me for clothes again, the king's soldiers will beat you, arrest you, and kill you. Get away from here!"

While Krishna's request was very polite and gentle, the washerman's response was very rude. He publicly ridiculed Krishna with loud, angry,

harsh, and insulting words. There were many washermen in Mathura, but this person happened to be the king's washerman, and thus was very arrogant.

Hearing the washerman's malicious words, Krishna effortlessly beheaded him merely with His fingertips. The Lord doesn't have to exert Himself to punish the arrogant. The washerman's assistants, seeing his untimely end, dropped their bundles of clothes on the spot and ran away in different directions. An effulgence (the soul) emerged from the washerman's body and merged with Lord Krishna. Thus, the Lord delivered him. Then Krishna, Balarama, and the other cowherds moved on after dressing themselves elegantly.

How merciful is Krishna! Even though the rude washerman insulted Krishna, yet He mercifully liberated him.

The Lord is kind enough to give us opportunities to serve Him. We need to be eager enough to grab them.

Krishna Blesses the Weaver

After Krishna liberated the washerman, he continued touring Mathura. He then came upon a weaver. Out of fear of Kamsa, this weaver had never gone to Vrindavan. But he had heard of its splendid atmosphere, and the miracles performed by the Lord from his companions who had

visited Vrindavan. Thus, anxious to see the Lord, he finally met young Krishna and Balarama.

Feeling great affection for the young brothers, the weaver dressed Them in soft silk clothes embedded with jewels. He offered Them exquisite armlets, bracelets, and earrings that perfectly suited Their complexions. The ornaments were suitable for the occasion too, because Krishna and Balarama would soon fight Kamsa's wrestlers, and these soft ornaments wouldn't hurt Their bodies.

The brothers looked resplendent. Pleased with the weaver's selfless service, Krishna blessed him to attain a cowherd's form in the spiritual world where he would enjoy varieties of divine pastimes.

In his past life the weaver had lived in Mithila. He was a great devotee and an expert weaver too. He had stitched extremely fine garments for Rama and Lakshmana to wear on Their wedding day. Seeing Rama and Lakshmana, who were more handsome than millions of cupids, the noble-hearted weaver desired to personally dress the two Lords with his own hands. Understanding His devotee's wish, Lord Rama decided to fulfil it. Thus, Rama and Lakshmana again appeared as Krishna and Balarama in Mathura, and gave Their devotee a chance to personally dress Them.

The Lord remembers the heartfelt desires of His devotees and fulfils them.

The washerman in Mathura arrogantly refused to serve Krishna, an opportunity that every devotee eagerly desires. On the other hand, the weaver joyfully dressed and adorned Krishna. Krishna reciprocated differently each time. But when He punishes someone, does it mean that He hates them? No, even His punishment is His protection. To know how, read the next shloka and the stories.

6. YOUR DEAREST FRIEND

भोक्तारं यज्ञतपसां सर्वलोकमहेश्वरम् ।
सुहृदं सर्वभूतानां ज्ञात्वा मां शान्तिमृच्छति ॥

bhoktaram yajna-tapasam
sarva-loka-mahesvaram
suhrdam sarva-bhutanam
jnatva mam santim rcchati ॥ (5.29) ॥

Who do you think is your best friend? Obviously, the one who is your well-wisher at all times, right? What if that person is the most powerful and the wealthiest person as well? Well, that personality is none other than Krishna.

In this shloka Krishna says: “I am the supreme enjoyer of all sacrifices, supreme proprietor of all planets and the dearest friend and well-wisher of all living beings. One who knows this about Me attains supreme happiness and peace.”

Krishna is the well-wisher of not only His devotees, but of demons too. Let’s read the stories of the two demons who tried to kill Krishna but were ironically liberated by His kindness.

Monstrous Mother

Once, a demoness named Putana was sent by Kamsa to kill baby Krishna in Gokula. Upon entering Gokula, Putana changed her form to that of a beautiful, motherly woman.

Seeing her, the innocent ladies thought that Goddess Lakshmi had come to see her husband Narayana who was being worshipped in the house of King Nanda. Everyone trusted her beyond doubt. Although Putana's heart was fierce and cruel, she presented herself like an affectionate mother. She resembled a sharp sword in a soft sheath.

She soon entered King Nanda's house without anyone's permission. Overwhelmed by her beauty, and apparent motherly love, Mother Yashoda also didn't stop her. Putana went into the inner chambers and saw baby Krishna sleeping in His cot, with His unlimited power covered like fire under ashes.

Putana knew that this wasn't an ordinary child, but was bent upon fulfilling her purpose. She took Krishna on her lap, just as a fool places a sleeping snake on one's lap, thinking it to be a rope.

The fierce demoness then started feeding her own milk to baby Krishna. With an evil intention to kill Krishna, Putana had smeared dangerous poison on her breast. That poison was so intense that even touching it could cause death. As soon as Krishna took hold of her breast, He squeezed it hard with His tender hands. He then began sucking both the poison and her life from her.

Putana screamed out in severe pain, "Please leave me! Get away from me!" Perspiring, her eyes wide open and her arms and legs flying in all directions, she cried loudly. People began falling to the ground fearing thunderstorms and thunderbolts, such was the ruckus she created. Putana could not maintain her disguise any longer. She reverted to her original form of a fearsome demoness. Seeing her thus, everyone realised who she was.

In this way Putana lost her life. She fell down in the pasturing ground and smashed all the trees up to twelve miles. Krishna was fearlessly playing on Putana's huge body. The simple-hearted gopis immediately picked Him up, and performed some rituals for Krishna's safety. Mother Yashoda fed Krishna her milk and then laid Him in bed.

By Krishna's touch, Putana's body was purified, and she was freed of all her sins. When the people of Vrindavan burnt her dead body, the smoke that emanated was so sweetly fragrant that people who were miles away could smell it.

Initially, Krishna was angry at Putana, because she had planned to kill many infants. However, He thought that Putana at least pretended to have the sentiments of a mother. Just seeing this, Krishna elevated her to the position of a motherly nurse to assist Mother Yashoda in Goloka Vrindavan. How can one find a person more merciful than Krishna? As the supreme well-wisher of all, His ultimate disposition towards all is 'Mercy'.

Krishna tries to find some reason to shower His mercy even on demons.

A Haunted Cart Attacks God

Utkacha was the son of the powerful demon named Hiranyaksha. He was immensely strong and was proud of his strength. Once, Utkacha went to the hermitage of a sage named Lomasa. To show off his great strength, he randomly started uprooting trees here and there.

Seeing him creating an unnecessary disturbance, the sage cursed him, "O evil-hearted one! Because you are so proud of your bodily strength, I curse you to become body-less!"

Utkacha's body at once fell away, just as a snake's old skin falls away. He became a ghostly being without a body. Utkacha realised

his mistake, and fell at Lomasa's feet. "O great sage, I did not know your power. Please forgive me and give me back my body," he begged. Lomasa replied, "Only the dust of Lord Krishna's lotus feet can liberate you from this ghostly life."

After this, Utkacha, wandering as a ghost, made friends with another demoniac person named Kamsa who was the cruel maternal uncle of Lord Krishna. Kamsa sent many of his demoniac friends to find and kill Krishna. Utkacha also arrived in Gokula to kill Krishna.

In King Nanda's courtyard, the demon entered a household cart loaded with many vessels made of gold, silver and brass. In Sanskrit, a cart is called shakata, and a demon is called asura. Therefore, Utkacha is also known as Shakatasura – the cart

demon. No one noticed Shakatasura, as he was invisible. He waited for an opportunity to kill Krishna.

At that time, Krishna was just three months old. Mother Yashoda laid Krishna down under the household cart that the ghost Utkacha had entered. She also lay down besides the child until He was asleep. When she saw that Krishna was fast asleep, she got up very gently and went back to attend to some guests. Some children who were playing nearby observed Krishna as He slept peacefully.

Because of Shakatasura, the wheels of the cart began to sink into the ground. Shakatasura intended to fall on Krishna and kill Him. But baby Krishna awoke and cried, as is usual for an infant, for His mother's milk. Mother Yashoda was busy with guests at that time, and couldn't hear the child crying. As an infant, Krishna angrily threw His little legs upwards in the air. The red sole of Krishna's soft foot touched the cart with the gesture of a kick.

Although Krishna's foot was as tender as a newly grown leaf, His kick turned the cart upside down and completely dismantled it. The wheels and axle of the cart were dislocated, its handle was broken, and all the utensils on it were scattered here and there. Thus, the demon in the cart died.

Shakatasura had entered the cart invisibly and was destroyed invisibly.

No one had noticed him. When the cart broke into pieces, Shakatasura left his subtle ghostly body and attained a pure spiritual body. He respectfully bowed down before Lord Krishna. In a chariot pulled by a hundred horses, he went to Krishna's abode - Goloka Vrindavan in the spiritual world. Such is the mercy of the Supreme Lord Krishna. Krishna 'punishes' the demons so that they simply get liberated!

If Krishna is so merciful to demons, just imagine how merciful He would be towards His devotees.

Lord Krishna is supremely kind for He is the well-wisher of all. He liberated both Putana and Shakatasura, the demons who intended to kill Him. If Krishna gives such treatment to demons, the treatment He gives to His devotees has to be super special, right? So, let's pray to Him with all our heart and experience His sweet friendship. In the last six shlokas and stories related to them, we came to know a lot about the Lord. Now let's see how we can develop knowledge about God.

7. FAITH IN THE GURU

श्रद्धावाँल्लभते ज्ञानं तत्परः संयतेन्द्रियः ।
ज्ञानं लब्ध्वा परां शान्तिमचिरेणाधिगच्छति ॥

sraddhaval labhate jnanam
tat-parah sam yatendriyah
jnanam labdhva param shantim
acirenadhigacchati ॥ (4.39) ॥

Who do you think among the following is indeed more knowledgeable:

(a) A school topper who gets excellent grades but is very proud, arrogant and refuses to help anyone; or,

(b) A humble student who studies sincerely, and helps others to the best of his/her ability, but doesn't score top marks in class?

Acquiring knowledge is not just about gathering some information and becoming a scholar. Real knowledge requires humility, good conduct, and respect for teachers.

In this *shloka*, Lord Krishna says, "One who has faith (*shraddha*), devotion and self-control can easily gain knowledge, and thus attain peace."

Here are some stories of great people who had deep faith in their *gurus* and thus attained knowledge.

The Uneducated Scholar

At the holy place of Sri Rangam in South India, there lived a simple brahmana. He used to visit the temple daily and attempt to recite the Bhagavad Gita with great joy. However, as he had not had formal

schooling, he couldn't pronounce the words correctly. People mocked, criticised and laughed at him, but he did not take offense. Neither was he discouraged. As he continued reading, he would get goosebumps, and tears of joy would well up in his eyes.

At that time, Lord Chaitanya Mahaprabhu, an incarnation of Lord Krishna, who was touring South India, visited the very same temple. Upon seeing the brahmana, He asked him, "My dear friend, why are you crying? Surely, your tears aren't due to any pain or distress. Please tell me, which part of the Bhagavad Gita gives you such joy?"

The brahmana innocently replied, "I am an uneducated man. I don't know the meaning of the words I read. Sometimes I pronounce them correctly and sometimes not, but still I read the Bhagavad Gita

only to honour my guru's instructions. Whenever I open the Gita, I see Lord Krishna driving Arjuna's chariot, taking the reins in his hands. I feel so delighted seeing how affectionate the Lord is towards His devotees."

Appreciating the brahmana's submissiveness to his guru, and his love for Krishna, Lord Chaitanya continued, "You are the best reader of the Bhagavad Gita. Whatever you know constitutes the real essence of the Gita." Speaking thus, Lord Chaitanya embraced him.

Lord Chaitanya was actually Lord Krishna Himself who came in the form of a sanyasi. By the Lord's mercy, this understanding was revealed to the brahmana. He caught the Lord's feet and expressed his feelings, "Upon seeing You, my happiness knows no bounds. You are the same Lord Krishna!"

Scholarship isn't essential for understanding the scriptures, but faith in the guru along with devotion to God is.

The Service of a Scholar

In ancient India, there once lived a great scholar named Dasarathi. He was a disciple of the great saint Ramanuja Acharya. Once, Dasarathi asked Ramanuja to explain the meaning of the final instruction of Lord Krishna in the Bhagavad Gita.

At that same time, Ramanuja's sister, Atulai arrived distressed at the scene. Seeing his sister in anxiety, Ramanuja asked Atulai, "What happened? Why are you so upset?"

Atulai replied, "Dear brother, my father has sent me here. At my father-in-law's house, daily I had to collect water from a lake which was over two miles away. I brought water twice a day. But the road to the lake was very rough and deserted. Therefore, I get scared and also really exhausted with the effort."

Ramanuja listened patiently, while Atulai continued, "I told my mother-in-law about these difficulties. But, rather than sympathising with me, she became enraged and told me to get a servant from my father's house for the job. Having received such ruthless treatment, I returned to my father's house, and he suggested that I approach you for help."

Ramanuja Acharya immediately responded, "Dear sister, please don't worry. I will send along with you a brahmana who will fetch water for you, and will cook food as well." Saying this, he glanced at the scholarly Dasarathi, indicating that he was supposed to accompany Atulai as a servant.

Dasarathi gladly followed Atulai to her father-in law's house. There, he began working in the kitchen with great care and attention. In this way, six months passed by.

One day, an assembly of people gathered in the village to attend a lecture by a great scholar. Dasarathi was also among the crowd. In his talk, the speaker gave some faulty explanations of a Sanskrit shloka. Dasarathi couldn't restrain himself after hearing such misinterpretations. He stood up and pointed out those errors.

At this, the speaker got furious and shouted, "Stop, you fool! How can a servant like you explain the scriptures? Go back to the kitchen and display your talents there."

Without being annoyed or discouraged, Dasarathi calmly went on explaining the shloka's correct meaning. His flawless presentation based on many scriptures, left everyone in the assembly, including the angered speaker, speechless. Realising his mistake, the speaker begged his pardon and fell at Dasarathi's feet.

The speaker asked, "How is it that such a learned scholar and devotee as yourself is doing such menial work in the kitchen?"

Dasarathi replied, "I am simply following the order of my guru."

When all the people learned that he was Dasarathi, the famous devotee-scholar, together, they went to Sri Rangam and met Ramanuja Acharya. They said in unison, "O great saint, it is improper for your worthy disciple to serve in the kitchen any longer. He is so knowledgeable, yet his heart is free of any pride. Please allow us to bring him back to you."

Ramanuja Acharya was very pleased to hear the people praising his disciple in such a way. He replied, "I shall come with you to bring back Dasarathi!"

Ramanuja Acharya then personally went to fetch Dasarathi. Dasarathi bowed down to Ramanuja, who then embraced and blessed him. Together, they returned to Sri Rangam. Ramanuja Acharya then explained to Dasarathi, Lord Krishna's final instruction to Arjuna in the Bhagavad Gita, which reveals how a devotee completely takes shelter of the Lord. By his selfless and humble service, Dasarathi received the learnings of the Bhagavad Gita from his guru.

A true disciple doesn't doubt his guru's instructions, but accepts them with faith.

The uneducated brahmana followed the instructions of his guru although others mocked him. Dasarathi took up the menial services Ramanuja Acharya assigned to him although he was a great scholar. In this way, obeying and keeping strong faith in the instructions of teachers enable us to become recipients of divine knowledge.
Apart from faith in our guru, what else is needed to acquire knowledge? Yes, you guessed it right. Devotion to God! That's our next topic.

8. DEVOTION GIVES KNOWLEDGE

भक्त्या मामभिजानाति यावान्यश्चास्मि तत्त्वतः ।
ततो मां तत्त्वतो ज्ञात्वा विशते तदनन्तरम् ॥

bhaktya mam abhijanati
yavan yash chasmi tattvatah
tato mam tattvato jnatva
vishate tad-anantaram ॥ (18.55) ॥

What is the qualification to know God? Wealth, beauty, scholarship, strength? Actually, none of these!

In this shloka, Lord Krishna teaches us the real qualification to know Him, "Only by loving devotion unto Me does one truly know Me. By thus knowing Me, My devotee always thinks of Me and comes to Me."

If we have love and devotion for God, we can easily understand Him, and explain His greatness to others as well. Without devotion, no one can attain knowledge of God or the ability to write or speak about God. Here are some stories for you to help you appreciate this shloka better.

The Five-year-old Guru of a Scholar

About nine centuries ago, in Sri Rangam, a holy place in Southern India, there lived a five-year-old child named Parashara.

One day a famous scholar named Digvijay Pandit arrived at Sri Rangam. He was a great champion of logic, grammar, and philosophy. He travelled throughout India challenging scholars to debate. He gained much wealth and fame by defeating many scholars in debates. He always had four strong men carry him in a

beautifully decorated palanquin from town to town, city to city. He had brahmanas chanting mantras and shlokas loudly as he travelled. There was no question that he couldn't answer. Whenever he arrived at any place, all the scholars would run away in fear of a challenge.

At Sri Rangam, little Parashara ran up to him and said "Sir, I have a question for you."

He looked down from his palanquin and said, "I am the champion scholar of the world. You are just a child. Go away."

Parashara argued, "But I have a question for you."

He said "Your mother's milk is still on your lips. Out from here, debating is serious stuff."

The little boy said, "If you're enlightened, why are you putting so much emphasis on the size of my body? I am not just my body. Please answer my question."

Exasperated, the Pandit asked, "What is your question?"

The little boy picked up a handful of sand. He held it right in front of the Pandit's face and said, "Tell me sir, how many grains of sand are there in my hand?"

The scholar was speechless. He had never been asked such a question.

Then little Parashara spoke, "A person with real knowledge sees God in everyone's heart. Such a person is like a tree with delicious fruits. A tree that has good fruits bows down. Similarly, if you are not humble before God and His devotees,then all your knowledge is as worthless as this handful of sand."

One who is humble learns even from younger people.

A Commentary by God's Grace

Once, the King of Jaipur was challenged by some scholars. They said, "Your Gaudiya Vaishnavism school is not authentic. Although you have commentaries (explanations) on the scriptures like the Bhagavad Gita, Srimad Bhagavatam and the Upanishads, you don't have a commentary on the Vedanta Sutras written by Sage Vyasa."

The king really wished to respond to this challenge and establish the authenticity of the Gaudiya Vaishnava school (*sampradaya*). He was reminded of his guru, Srila Vishvanath Chakravarti Thakur, a great devotee of Lord Krishna. Vishvanath Chakravarti was a great author who had written many devotional books. The king then sent word to his guru asking for his help. But at that time, Vishvanath Chakravarti was very old and could not travel to Jaipur in person. Therefore, he sent his scholarly disciple Baladev Vidyabhushan instead.

Baladev Vidyabhushan understood the situation. But he hesitated, thinking, *How can I write a commentary on the Vedanta Sutras? Vyasadev, the author of the Vedanta Sutras, has already written a commentary in the form of Srimad Bhagavatam. When the author himself has written a commentary, how can I write it again? But since the king is so worried about establishing the authenticity of our Vaishnava school, and they all are insisting, maybe I should give it a try.*

Thinking thus, Baladev Vidyabhushan went to the temple of Lord Govindaji. He prayed to the Lord for some direction and fell at His feet. In sanction, Lord Govindaji's garland fell on him. Lord Govinda thus blessed His dear devotee with the expertise and ability to write the commentary. Baladev Vidyabhushan felt

extremely grateful and thus wrote the commentary. He was given a month's time to write the commentary, but Baladev completed it much sooner.

Baladev Vidyabhushan declared, "What I have written as the commentary to the Vedanta Sutra are not my words; I have written whatever Lord Govindaji made me write. Therefore, this commentary will be known as the Govinda-bhashya."

Govinda-bhashya, that was personally blessed and inspired by Lord Govinda in reciprocation to the devotion of Baladev Vidyabhushan, eventually became a famous and profound explanation on the Vedanta Sutra.

Krishna is very eager to reveal rare knowledge to His devotees who surrender unto Him.

Proud Digvijay Pandit who had no devotion towards the Lord, was defeated by a child in a debate. But Baladev Vidyabhushan, who had great devotion, was empowered by the Lord to write a great scholarly commentary and uphold the credibility of a Vaishnava school. So, it's devotion that provides knowledge and at times, is more important than knowledge itself.

So, children, now you know a lot about God and also learnt how to reach Him. Would you like to know something about yourself, and the nature? Then read the last two shlokas and the connected stories.

9. THE SOUL IS ETERNAL

वासांसि जीर्णानि यथा विहाय
नवानि गृह्णाति नरोऽपराणि ।
तथा शरीराणि विहाय जीर्णा-
न्यन्यानि संयाति नवानि देही

vasamsi jirnani yatha vihaya
navani grihnati naro 'parani
tatha sharirani vihaya jirnany
anyani samyati navani dehi ॥ (2.22) ॥

Do you know what the terms 'birth' and 'death' mean? Birth basically means that a person has entered a new body. And death means that the person left the body to enter another body. Birth and death exist only for the body and not for the person or soul that lives within the body. While the body is temporary, the soul is eternal and deathless. This is one of the major and first teachings of the Bhagavad Gita.

In this shloka, Krishna describes the eternal nature of the soul with an example. "Just as one leaves old and worn-out clothes and wears new clothes, similarly, a person (the soul) gives up an old and worn-out body (death), and enters a new body (birth)."

This concept, though deep in meaning, can be understood easily with stories. Why wait then? Go ahead!

The Boy Who Gave Joy and Sorrow

Once there was a king called Chitraketu who ruled the Surasena province. During his reign, the Earth was prosperous. He was handsome, kind, educated, famous and wealthy. However, he was very sad because he didn't have a child despite having ten million wives.

One day, Sage Angira came to King Chitraketu's palace. Chitraketu welcomed the sage with due respect and warmth. Sage Angira asked Chitraketu, "Dear King, is everything well with you? I see that your mind is restless. Your pale face reflects your sorrow."

Chitraketu replied, "Nothing is unknown to holy sages like you. Yet, let me tell you the cause of my sadness. My wealth and kingdom do not please me, because I have no child. Please help me beget a son who can rule the kingdom after me."

Angira then conducted a sacrifice. From the sacrificial fire, a celestial being emerged and offered a pot of sweets. Angira gave that sweet to Kritadyuti, the first wife of Chitraketu. As she consumed it, she was told that by its power she would soon give birth to a child.

Angira then informed Chitraketu, "Your son will be the cause of both joy and sorrow for you." Angira then left. Chitraketu interpreted Angira's words in this way: "My son's birth will certainly cause happiness. But, because he will be my only son, he will probably be proud of his great wealth and empire, and may not be very obedient. Thus, he might cause distress. But that is alright."

After some time, Kritadyuti gave birth to a beautiful son. Everyone celebrated this long-awaited occasion. Chitraketu's joy knew no bounds. He generously donated gold, silver, ornaments, garments, villages, horses, and so on, just like a cloud pours rain.

Chitraketu's affection for his son and Kritadyuti grew day by day. He slowly began neglecting his other wives. This made the remaining queens envious. They thought, *The new-born child is the cause of our sorrow. Let us kill him.* Their jealousy made them lose their minds, and do the unthinkable. They poisoned the child to death.

Unaware of the sinful act of her co-wives, Kritadyuti thought that her son had been sleeping for a long time. Later, she sent her maid to wake him up, only to realise that the child was dead. Shocked at seeing the lifeless boy, she cried profusely and fell to the ground unconscious. All the palace residents gathered there and began to cry. The queens who had poisoned him also cried pretentiously.

When Chitraketu heard of his son's death, he became almost blind with grief. Slipping and falling, he approached the dead child and fell unconscious.

At that time, Sage Angira arrived there along with Narada Muni. Narada Muni said, "As sand particles on a seashore come together and get separated by the force of waves, the living beings also sometimes come together and get separated by the force of time. We were not together before birth, and will not be together after death. God brings people together and disperses them as they deserve."

Narada Muni then spoke to the soul of the dead boy, "Dear child, just look at your father and mother. Everyone is grief-stricken because of your passing away. Re-enter your body and enjoy life with your relatives. Accept your father's royal throne and be a good king to your people." So saying, he brought the son back to life with his mystic powers.

The boy spoke, "O great sage, in which birth were these persons my parents? I have been wandering in the bodies of devas, animals, and human beings. In many lifetimes, I had many parents from different species. In different births, different people become our friends, relatives, enemies, well-wishers, and so on. All these relationships are valid only when one is within a body. But no one is permanently

related." Saying this, the boy again left, and people saw only his dead body.

Chitraketu and all others were amazed on hearing the bitter facts of life taught by the child. Giving up their sadness, they dutifully arranged for the funeral ceremony of the dead boy, as a matter of custom. Kritadyuti's co-wives were ashamed of their sinful act. They atoned for the killing of the child on the banks of the Yamuna River as directed by brahmanas.

Thereafter, Chitraketu chanted a mantra given by Narada Muni continuously for one week. His mind thus calmed down and he became increasingly attached to Lord Vishnu. Eventually, the Lord appeared before him and blessed him.

One shouldn't get too elated in happiness, or too depressed in distress. Both situations are temporary.

The Truths of Life

There was once a great king named Suyajna who ruled the Ushinara province. Once, while fighting in battle, unfortunately, the courageous king died at the hands of his enemies.

At the time of sunset, King Suyajna's queens ran to the battlefield and saw the dead body of their beloved husband. They cried piteously for him. They said, "O lord, now that you are killed, we are also as good as dead. Cruel destiny has taken you away from our sight. You were a great husband and our most sincere friend. We cannot

exist without you. We will also die now, and follow you to serve you wherever you go." Thus, they fell at his feet with tears, pounding their chests.

The queens kept crying and wouldn't allow anyone to take the body for cremation. Soon their cries reached the abode of Yama, the Lord of Death, who punishes sinful people in hell. To advice the queens of Suyajna, Lord Yama personally appeared before them in the form of a boy.

The boy then spoke to the queens, "Alas, it is amazing that these people, older than me, who have seen hundreds of births and deaths, are still confused. For anyone who is born, death is unavoidable. The soul is different from the body, which differs from species to species and appears and disappears by karma. The soul identifies with the body only due to ignorance. Still the relatives of a dead person cannot understand this. Those who are really wise know that the soul is eternal and the body is temporary. Hence, do not lament."

Although Yama himself was educating them in the form of the boy, the queens didn't stop their lamentation. So, Yama narrated a story, "Once there lived a hunter who would kill the birds in the forest. One day, he saw a pair of kulinga birds and captured the female bird in his net. Seeing his wife in danger and being unable to release her, the male bird cried, 'Destiny is merciless. What is the use of my life, after my wife's death? Let me also die! The baby birds are helpless. How shall I maintain these fledglings who haven't developed wings?' As the male bird was thus crying, the hunter shot him down with his arrow."

Lord Yama concluded, "Dear queens, even if you lament for hundreds of years, your husband will not come back to life. In the meantime, your lives will be finished. So better stop wasting your time crying, and instead focus on devotion to Lord Vishnu."

Everyone was struck with wonder at the words of the boy. Yama then disappeared, and Suyajna's relatives were able to conduct the funeral ceremony.

Emotions are common when we lose our dear ones.
But that shouldn't make one dysfunctional.

Both King Chitraketu and the wives of King Suyajna were pained when their beloved relatives left their bodies. But, wise devotees namely Narada, Angira and Yama explained to them the truth of life. Yes, it's very painful when one's dear friends or relatives die, and one naturally feels for them. But one shouldn't become demotivated or dysfunctional at that time. Instead, one must try to accept the truth and move on with one's responsibilities.

10. NATURE IS UNDER GOD'S CONTROL

मयाध्यक्षेण प्रकृतिः सूयते सचराचरम् ।
हेतुनानेन कौन्तेय जगद्विपरिवर्तते ॥

mayadhyakshena prakritih
suyate sa-characharam
hetunanena kaunteya
jagad viparivartate ॥ (9.10) ॥

Can stones float on water? Can a child lift a mountain? No way, right? Nature and its various elements have certain properties that are unchangeable. However, only the person who gave them those properties can change them if He so desires.

Krishna says in this shloka, "This material nature is working under My direction, and is producing all moving and stationary beings. All changes that the material nature undergoes or causes are due to Me."

Thus, the material elements like earth, water, air, fire and sky – all work under the direction of the Lord, who can give them their characteristics and change them if needed. Here are two beautiful tales of the Lord for you to understand this better.

The Floating Stones

Hearing that Sita Devi was in Lanka, Lord Rama wanted to rescue her immediately. Lord Rama took the huge army of monkeys and went to the shore of the ocean that stood between Lanka and them. It was a big task for the millions of monkeys to cross the ocean. Lord Rama wondered how the crossover would be possible and appealed to the ocean god, Samudra.

After a long time, the ocean god finally rose from the ocean. He seemed like the bright sun at dawn. He wore a red dress with a garland of red flowers and his eyes appeared like lotuses. He wore a flower crown and a prominent jewel around his neck. He was surrounded by many river goddesses. He folded his hands and spoke humbly, "My dear Lord

Rama, every element has its natural state, therefore it won't be possible for me to change the state of this ocean. Still, I can tell You the means by which You can cross me along with Your army. You can construct a bridge over me, which I will sustain against my nature. I can assure you that the fierce creatures in the ocean wouldn't disturb Your army. O Rama, although You can easily cross the ocean without even making a bridge, still I request You to construct the bridge so that future generations can know and witness Your greatness through this superhuman activity of making stones float on water."

Thus, assured by the ocean god, Lord Rama was pleased. The monkeys then jumped joyfully and began their work. Soon, there were thousands of trees and massive heaps of rocks piled on the beach. One of the monkeys, named Nala, was a good architect. Nala told the monkeys to throw the rocks and trees into the sea. And they threw huge rocks that created huge splashes of water. However, instead of sinking, the rocks magically started floating on water. Binding together trees and rocks with creepers, the monkcys built a huge bridge towards Lanka.

Finally, in five days the monkeys constructed an enormous bridge that stretched several miles up to the shores of Lanka. Lord Rama and Lakshmana mounted the backs of Hanuman and Angada and reached the shores of Lanka with the help of the amazing bridge. In this way by the power of Lord Rama, even the heavy, sinkable stones began to float on water. This superhuman deed of Lord Rama has been praised ever since.

The Lord performs superhuman acts to please His devotees.

Big Hill on a Small Finger

Once, Indra, the king of heaven and the lord of rains, became proud of his power and position. Taking note of this unnecessary pride, Lord Krishna decided to stop the traditional worship of Indra in Vrindavan. Instead, he initiated the worship of Govardhan Hill. The cowherd community in Vrindavan celebrated this new Govardhan puja in Vrindavan with great joy.

But Indra became furious and caused a devastating downpour in Vrindavan. Forgetting that his position was only due to Krishna's mercy, he arrogantly criticised Krishna and decided to destroy the supposed pride of the people of Vrindavan.

Indra then sent the dense Samvartaka clouds, accompanied by seven types of fierce winds that can destroy the entire world. There were many colourful clouds – black, yellow, green, red, camphor, blue lotus – moving in the sky like huge elephants moving side by side. With wild lightning, thunder and winds, the Samvartaka clouds poured rain continuously in Vrindavan like piercing arrows, as thick as pillars, along with big and heavy pieces of ice. The torrential rain falling from the sky appeared like the long hanging branches of a banyan tree.

All the lands were soon filled with water. The cows were severely tormented by cold and tried to shelter their calves underneath their bodies. The disturbed cowherd community approached the palace of King Nanda to seek Lord Krishna's shelter.

It is Krishna's solemn vow to protect His devotees who exclusively take His shelter in all circumstances. Krishna decided to counteract the situation by displaying His omnipotence. By His divine power, the rain temporarily ceased to fall over the path that extended from King Nanda's house to the Govardhan Hill. Krishna ran swiftly from the porch of His house to the Govardhan Hill without a single raindrop falling on Him.

Just as a child picks up a mushroom, or an elephant lifts a clump of grass, Krishna effortlessly picked up the Govardhan Hill which was touching the clouds. Thus, Krishna became Giridhari, the lifter of the hill. The hill rose as if it had wings. All the devatas, except Indra, became joyful and began praising this feat. Flowers fell from the trees on Govardhan representing his laughter since he was being touched by Krishna's hand. Giriraja seemed to celebrate the destruction of Indra's fame.

King Nanda, Mothers Yashoda and Rohini, the gopas and gopis, including thousands of cows, calves, bulls, buffaloes and the entire cowherd community gathered under Govardhan. Ordinarily, all of them would not have fit under the base of a medium-sized hill like Govardhan. However, through the power of Krishna's touch, Govardhan expanded to thirty-two miles so that all of them could be sheltered comfortably under him. A chunk of earth fell and formed a natural boundary wall around the perimeter of Govardhan, and prevented the water from entering this periphery. Sheshnag had coiled himself around Govardhan to stop the water from flowing under the hill. Sudarshan Chakra, as brilliant as ten million suns, hovered above the hill and drank up the falling streams of water. Thus, not a blade of grass moved in Vrindavan due to Indra's fierce rain.

After seven days, when the efforts of Indra became futile, the sky became clear and the sun began to shine. While these seven days were like seven yugas of intense pain for Indra, they were like seven joy-filled hours for the residents of Vrindavan. Krishna then placed Govardhan back on the ground where He had stood earlier.

Whether the Lord protects or punishes, all His activities are merciful and enchanting.

Since the Lord controls nature, He alone can make stones float and can lift a big hill on His little finger. He even chastises Devas if they go astray due to pride or greed.
Krishna is the storehouse of all superpowers and He makes use of His powers to protect His devotees and make them happy. So, let's make sure we pray to Him, serve Him and most importantly befriend Him!

The Power of Jnana- Knowledge

Wow! You did it! From the episode of the Uneducated Scholar in Sri Rangam to a Big Hill on a Small Finger in Vrindavan, you have covered all these simple, interesting and inspiring tales. Travelling page to page to get more jnana about the Lord you didn't tire. Instead, you still want more.

So, here's a promise. We're bringing to you THE GITA WISDOM TALES 3 - KARMA packed and charged with more of such sweet, unheard and jaw-dropping stories for you to treasure, and learn the smart art of doing your work in this world. Narrate these stories to your family and friends and help spread the power of jnana or knowledge.

Until then, happy reading, young friends!

- Gauranga Darshan Das

Author's Profile

Gauranga Darshan Das, a disciple of His Holiness Radhanath Swami, is an educator, TEDx speaker and a spiritual author of over thirty-two books. He holds a master's degree from the Indian Institute of Science, Bangalore. He is a resident of the ISKCON Govardhan Ecovillage (GEV) and serves as the dean of the Bhaktivedanta Vidyapitha. He is also a member of the ISKCON Board of Examinations and GEV Administrative Council.

He regularly delivers online and residential discourses for children and adults in various forums, including temples, ashrams, schools, colleges, corporate events and platforms such as TEDx, Defence Research and Development Organization (DRDO), Rotary Club, Hindustan Times, etc. He is a regular speaker on Hare Krsna TV. He has conducted over forty-five online courses (www.vidyapitha.in) and over 7500 hours of lectures. He travels to various places in India, Australia, United States, etc., to teach and inspire spiritual seekers.

Some of his literary contributions include the *Subodhini* series of study guides, the *Pravaha* series of storybooks, self-enrichment books like *Disapproved but Not Disowned*, children's book series like *Bhagavatam Tales* and *Gita Wisdom Tales*, and shloka compilations like the *Ratnamala* series. He runs a monthly ezine called *Bhagavata Pradipika* whilst penning thought-inspiring articles for international and Indian *Back to Godhead* magazines.

Find more about him on www.gaurangdarshan.com